Evil May-day, &c

William Allingham

Nabu Public Domain Reprints:

You are holding a reproduction of an original work published before 1923 that is in the public domain in the United States of America, and possibly other countries. You may freely copy and distribute this work as no entity (individual or corporate) has a copyright on the body of the work. This book may contain prior copyright references, and library stamps (as most of these works were scanned from library copies). These have been scanned and retained as part of the historical artifact.

This book may have occasional imperfections such as missing or blurred pages, poor pictures, errant marks, etc. that were either part of the original artifact, or were introduced by the scanning process. We believe this work is culturally important, and despite the imperfections, have elected to bring it back into print as part of our continuing commitment to the preservation of printed works worldwide. We appreciate your understanding of the imperfections in the preservation process, and hope you enjoy this valuable book.

To follow,
BY THE SAME,
In like form:

Ashby Manor: A Play.

Brambleberries.

BY

WILLIAM ALLINGHAM

London:
LONGMANS & Co., PATERNOSTER ROW.

[All rights reserved.]

To
MY CHILDREN.

CONTENTS.

	PAGE
Evil May-Day	1
In a Cottage Garden	31
"Everything passes and vanishes"	32
Sonnet: Daffodil	33
Ne quid nimis	33
The Honest Farmer	34
"See what lives of mortals are"	35
"Man's found by his event"	35
Sonnet: "Love after long"	36
"Why, yes,—we've pass'd a pleasant day"	36
A Sad Song	37
Sleepy	38
"Art thou Lord of the World?"	39
Sonnet: A Flower (in time of war)	40
"Deny not Love and Friendship"	40
News from Pannonia	41
Sonnet: A Nursery Rhyme for the Elders	58
The Funeral	59
No funeral gloom	60
"This patchwork world"	60
A Week-day Hymn	61
A Modern Pleasaunce	63
An Invitation	64
The First English Poet	65
Sonnet: In a Book of Maxims	69

CONTENTS.

	PAGE
The Stolen Path	70
Per Contra	72
Three Sisters	73
The Adventure of the Lamp	73
"Mine—mine—"	74
"I and my Love together"	75
"Who could say that Love is blind?"	75
Poesis Humana	76
Great Ancestry	78
"Autumn and Sunset now"	79
"Four ducks on a pond"	79
"Alas, friend"	80
Que sçais-je?	80
Equality at Home	81
A Reminiscence of the Isle of Man	81
Dreams	83
Vivant!	84
Birds' Names	85
"I'm but a lowly gooseberry"	86
Amy Margaret	87
"I saw a little Birdie fly"	87
A Mountain Round	88
John Clodd	90
Familiar Epistle to a Little Boy	92
The Winter Pear	98
"New Heavens and New Earth"	98
"When I was young"	99
Liber Loquitur	100

EVIL MAY-DAY.

Part I.

SUDDENLY, softly, I awoke from sleep;
My lattice open to the morning sun,
Call of a distant cuckoo, lyric notes
Of many a voice, leaf-whispers.
                                May, once more,
Her dewy fragrant kiss, and all the love
It wakes us to,—a joyous, beauteous world!
Long shadows lying on the luminous grass;
The lilac's purple honeycombs enswathed
In freshest foliage; snowy pear-tree bloom;
Birds on our daisied lawn, or flitting swift
Through floating under-boughs to elmtops fledged
Against the tenderly translucent sky;
And through the leafage glimpses of a realm
Of woodland slopes and vales, and distant hills
Of bright horizon. O the sweet old rapture!
May in my inmost soul awaking too.
This might be Earth's first morning, or the rise
Of that New Heav'n and Earth—
                                Ah pain! ah grief!
The happy wingèd thing afloat on air

Smit with a cruel pang, down-fluttering, drops,
Ev'n as my heart—
          They say "There is no God!"

  Evil May-day, by my account. Long since,
Whispers of bale were rife; dark prophecies
And dim forebodings brought a passing qualm,
A momentary shiver; that was all;
As peradventure may a man have heard
Rumour of pestilence in Eastern lands,
Of little import: "creeping westward" next:
"Within our country's border" (this is grave):
And then a pause, time slides, the man has turn'd
To his affairs and pleasures; when one day
What's this the mirror shows him?—Heaven and
    Hell!
The plague-spot on his tongue! His lot is drawn.

  Yes, look upon thy hands and touch thy head;
'Tis thou—that wakedst oft in other Mays,
Didst kneeling say thy pray'r, and look aloft
As into thy dear Father's face, and see
His handiwork all round thee, all done right.
The lilies of the field and the seven stars,
Beast, bird, and insect, and immortal Man;
"These are Thy glorious works, Parent of good!"—
"In wisdom hast Thou made them all."
                      Poor fool!
  Gaze round now on the sunshine and the grass,
Enjoy their brightness, hear the senseless birds

Chatter and chirp, and be thou merry too.
All's but a dream; and why torment thyself?
—Because the plague is come. The bird is hit.
A dream is *fled;* and now I wake aghast.
I see this world a body without soul;
I see the flow'rs and greenery of May
A garland on a corpse. "There is no God."

Nay, courage! let the fearful mood pass by.
Here is no plague. Behind these branching elms
Our shady lane winds to the village green,
Its ancient cottages, its ivied tower,
With graves of twenty generations. Hark!
The dial: sturdy Labour forth has trudged
With tools in hand; Age on his doorstep greets
The friendly sunshine; Childhood swarms to school
And hums like bees in clover, till the song
Heartily rises: and our week moves round,
As weeks and years and centuries have moved,
Over this English village in its vale,
Secluded from the world,—not separate.
There goes the flutter of a distant train
Speeding to the great city full of men
And men's accumulated thought and work,
With ships from every sea along her wharves.
Art thou delirious? or wilt thou count
All this, insanity—the varied life
In fields and cities, work and worship and love,
Whate'er binds men together, linking past,
Present, and future—

    O let be ! let be !
No form of speech can do me any good,
My own or other men's devisal, fresh
As primrose, venerable as churchyard yew.
Having heard sentence pass'd, no other words
Can carry meaning ; one brief dismal phrase
Knolls on the air—"No God !" and still—"No God !"

 Pretence of continuity ! talk, preach,
Write books ; build cities, churches, monuments ;
Patch up and varnish histories, pedigrees ;
Take childish titles, worship toyshop crowns ;
Sustain (save when alone or with a friend)
The masquerade of dignity ; pass on
Old phrases, teach them to the children ; make
Your little mark, or big, as one who scribes
Two letters, or full name, or date therewith,
Upon a tree, and dies, and in a while
The tree perishes also. Vain conceit !
Swim with me, fellow-bubbles, catch fine hues
And picture-like reflections, and then burst !
The swift stream flows, the shoreless sea of forms
Melting, reshaping, seeming (since our life
Is like a flash of lightning) permanent ;
But rolling ever from darkness into darkness.
GOD was behind that darkness once ;—that sea
His effluent power. But now, there is no God.

After the first sharp pain I wrote this down
To ease awhile my heart-ache. Count not these

But idle words ; for since I wotted first
Of my own being, never grief like that.
"Able to soothe all sadness but despair"
The poet sang . no finest solaces
Had any comfort. Through the dismal time
I dragged from sleep to sleep, groaning the while,
As one sore-wounded drags from pause to pause ;
And sleep was like a swoon, or else perturb'd
With shapeless terror.

     But sleep grew more calm
(I know not when or how began the change)—
And all things with it; wind and wave went down
And life took on its ordinary look
By slow gradations. All was as before ?
Not so. I was not in perpetual pain ;
Only half-paralysed. Month after month,
And after that sad year, another year,
And after this, another year. I went
And came and talk'd and laugh'd, like those around
  me ;
Only I recollected now and then,
And shiver'd, whispering to myself " No God."

 No God, no Soul : they are the self-same thought.
And I, that think it, turning into mire
To-morrow or next year, I care not much
What may befall a race of things like me,
A little better luck, a little worse,
As each flits by and vanishes for ever.

To-morrow will be nothing; and To-day
That leads to it, is next to nothing.   Go!
Laugh, weep, do what you will, eat, drink, and die—
The sad old phrase found true.
       Is't selfishness
Thus craves for God, that God may give us life
After this life?   New life be as it may,
That irks me nothing.   It is this my life
I would not lose, the life within this life.
And I have lost it, if there be no God.

EVIL MAY-DAY.

Part II.

OF all pathetic things the most is this—
    A happy bright-eyed Child, some four years old,
Making acquaintance with man's common world.
Joy, wonder, eager questionings; anon
An anxious look, a swift and wide-eyed stare
At his dear Oracle; and merry laughs
And low contented songs made by himself
Are his; and youthful strange imaginings!
And sometimes you may see those innocent eyes
Fix'd in a meditative trance, the while
He strives to see some vaguest vapoury form
Of thought within him.
                O this world of ours!

I am your Prophet, Priest, and Oracle,
My little Son; whatever I respond
Is fate. One only answer vexes you—
"I do not know." You try and try again
For something better, and are ill-content.
But often must you hear those baffling words;
And often must you say them to yourself
When manhood, which you deem omniscient,
Is yours in turn,--is like what we have found.

A Prophet's highest care—not to mislead
His neophyte. The dream, the phantasy
I put into his mind, is truth for him,
Until he finds it untrue. This young soul
Tremulous with wonder, curiosity,
Imagination, (look but in his face)
Drinks in the world through every joyful sense;
Sensation turns to thought, and thought revives
Sensation in the memory; thus is built
The body of the mind by slow degrees,
With order'd imagery, with habitudes
Of movement; and the little world it lives in
Is its own making chiefly. All the while,
The great world lives around it, and includes
It with the rest of things. A word of mine,
Be it the emptiest breath, can take firm shape
In my son's world; the herald's animals,
Insert them in his natural-history book,
Were just as credible as any there;
Angel is no whit harder to conceive
Than eagle, and a Heaven above the clouds
(Reach'd by balloon perhaps) much easier
Than suns and planets and space without a bound.

You shall not build a false world, little Son,
If skill of mine can sift the follies out
Men have mix'd up with everything. My care
Is less to teach than save you from being taught
Half-truths and falsehoods in your tender time

Beware, my Son, of words! The Human Race

Hath stored its wisdom there, its errors there,
Mistakes and follies and duplicities.
Of words false gods are made, each doom'd at last
A worn-out idol to the lumber-loft
Or trim museum,—concourse wonderful,
Superb, grotesque, pathetic, and obscene!

   Childhood will ask, "Who made all these things?"
    "GOD."
"Where does God live?"—suppose I point and say,
"On that high mountain top;" my child regards
The peak with joyful awe; but one day climbs
And finds a barren frosty crag,—nor heeds
The wide-spread glory of things encircling it.
He hears of Heaven above the clouds; his book
At school confutes it: starry heaven goes blank.
Words said to children can be only true,
Or not, in their direct and simple sense.
"At such and such a place, God walked with men,
They saw and heard Him; what he said and did
Is warrant for your duties and your hopes."
The warm young spirit trustfully accepts,
Lies down, uprises, in a full belief,
From day to day, for many days and years;
Till one day comes the question "Is this true?"
Nay, teach the plans, ways, character of God,
With Man's relations to Him thence deduced,
In any form of words you will: how fence
The fatal question out—"But is this true?"
The answer "No!" smites all truth to the ground,

The vine and prop together; Truth itself,
Immortal Truth, lies murder'd!
                                  Foolishness,
Dishonesty and cowardice of men,
What bitter pain, what cruel wrongs ye breed!
As if our case were not perplex'd enough,
And troublesome enough, and sad enough,
But we must writhe in self-inflicted pangs!

  But in the reign of Science you are born.
Theology, with pomp and riches yet,
Sits mumbling, droning, in his padded chair,
Gouty, asthmatic, ailing every way.
A young audacious voice rings through the land—
"Ask questions, men, where ye may hope reply
By gauge of human faculties, may test
Reply when found. First cause and final cause
In every case being out of reach, henceforth
Fix eye and thought upon the scrutable;
Travel, examine, and subdue throughout
The great domain of Science; step by step,
Link after link, trace, test, confirm and fix
The sequences of natural law; reduce
The complex to the simple; thus control,
So far as man may do so, human life,
The race itself; attain, whate'er it be,
No twilight Land of Dreams, Fool's Paradise,
Hid in a theologic labyrinth
Or metaphysic jungle. How sublime
In its simplicity, one single fact

In pure mechanic formula express'd
(Shall it be call'd *Vibration?*—possibly)
And all phenomena its aspects merely!
This we shall find at last."
                              And then? what then?
Are we at home henceforward in the world?
All comfortably settled in our minds,
Knowing the immortal truth—Vibration?
Shall we spoonfeed our babes on science-pap,
Till teeth find tougher work? train them to scan
The mechanism of all phenomena,
To measure and set it down in proper form,—
The *ne plus ultra* this, which cannot baulk?

  Again I say, Beware of words, my son.
Exact and systematic knowledge—good!
But now, of what? Of the true nature of things?
This is abjured. No step found possible
In that direction. Of phenomena?
"Surely" But I deny it: very close
We peer, and make our atoms very small,
Yet after all 'tis but the coarser part
Of any one phenomenon of nature
Which we can measure and make record of.
Science is measurement, no more, no less,
Whatever sauce we add. Minds wholly fill'd
With Physical Science (and a fond conceit
That they alone know Nature) miss and lose
The natural appearances of things
Beyond all common ignorance. Day and night,
Earth, ocean, sky, the seasons, peopled full

With countless forms of life ; a world imbued
With beauty and with wonder and with awe,
Powers inexpressible and infinite,
Whereto man's spirit exquisitely thrills,
Raised, rapt, and soaring on celestial wings,—
Which extasy begetteth Art in some,
In every sane soul Worship in some wise,
Voiceless or silent,—shall we see instead
The tall ghost of a pair of compasses
Stalking about a world of diagrams,
And algebraic regiments that march
And countermarch, and wheel ?
       O learn all this—
If so thou fail not to come back at last,
My son, to nature's own rich symbolism !
Value *appearances*, and study these
To see them well,—your first relationship,
Your last and truest too, with circumstance ;
More excellent by far to apprehend
Than all disclosures of analysis.
Upon the surface earthly Beauty blooms,
Yielding itself to every loving eye,
Known heavenly in its correspondences
When Seer or Poet comes ; immortal flow'r,
Beloved of Man's soul, no trivial thing,
No fleeting thing, as flimsy proverbs wail !
Inferior truths are good in their degree,
But the first-met is first, nor ever can
Be weigh'd or measured. That the world is fair
Concerns us more than that the world is round,

(Though this, like every truth, be well to know);
The rose, the primrose, and the hawthorn-flow'r,
The colours of the dawn or evening air,
The woodlands, and the mountains, and the meads,
Lakes, rivers, rivulets and rocky springs,
The varying ocean and the starry night,
Have in their beauty more significance
Than tabulated light-waves which impinge
On optic nerves and yield the brain a sense
Of red, blue, yellow—Science knows not how.
Science can but afford a pitying smile
If you forget that just where warmth begins
Of human interest in a question, there
Science stops short. And let her have the praise
Of keeping in her limit, if she keep,
And lack not limitation's humbleness.

Beware, I say, of words, warm, wide, and loose;
Beware of cold and rigid formulæ
No less: both full of power—they are not things,
Nor even thoughts, but shadowings-forth of thoughts,
Wearing a phantom dignity themselves.
True, that we think by these: most men by words,
The grave mathematician by his signs,
Expressing a mechanic universe,
Yet giving irrepressible Fancy room
To sport in magical curves and deem herself
Almost creative in mechanic wise,
Leaving out life and beauty merely. Words
Have melody and colour, and therewith

The Poet's art can build a lovelier world,
Nay, truer than the common, for the gold
Is smelted from the dross that made it dull.
Be ever thankful of poetic truth,
And hold it fast. Value *Appearances*,
And let *Imagination* teach their worth,
Counting this practical. A sane clear mind
To see, and to imagine, is a mind
Of noblest rank: learning will nourish it,
But not to any show of learning: such
Are Seers and Poets. Through appearances
Beheld with keen and sympathetic eyes
Imaginative insight pierces deep
To something secret,—not mechanical
But spiritual, and wholly beyond reach
Of Science, which too often is so vain
As therefore to deny it scornfully;
Spiritual, and not contain'd or circumscribed
In any science ever formulated,
Or any creed that is or will be made,
Or aught that eye can see, or ear can hear;
For subtler, dearer, more delicious beauty
Lives in the soul than in the outer world,
And therefore fact is poor to hopes and dreams,
Child-fancies beggar all the famous things.

Ah, might we trust the Poets all in all!
Too often they divert themselves and us
With gambols in the air. Amorous of words,
Temptable by a rhyme or phrase, they make
Language their end not means; or sometimes stoop

To stroke the public ear and give those jaws
The food they gape for.
                    Men, in short, my son,
Speak truth by most imperfect signs at best,
And with it many follies, many lies,
Deceiving or deceived, being only men,
Weak, wavering, limited. Yet Men alone
See, note, explore, make record of, would fain,
But cannot ever, comprehend the world,
Life being a mystery, not a mechanism;
Orderly miracle, where some men see
The order, some the wonder, most, and shape
Their diagrams, their phantasies; the Wise,
Wedding experience and imagination—
Both; and lift up their eyes and hands to GOD.

   As to the Future, that is God's affair.
I am not Ruler of the Universe,
Nor in His secrets; but I hold Him good,
His riches boundless, and His will to give.
Also that Man has share, whatever share,
In working out the Universal Plans,
And our own fate is partly in our power,
For each, for all; how far we cannot know.
This I do know, immortal thoughts alone,
Eternal things, have interest for my soul—
That which is truly me, my inmost self.

Man can help men, and also hinder them.
Men's evil and folly are to guard against,

Assuming many shapes; not dangerous least
In Books, pretended utterances of thought.
I say it who have loved books all my life.
The tongue may lie, or, self-deceiving, show
Folly as wisdom, may omit or add,
Transpose, misrepresent; more easily
The pen; and lo, by typographic art
What inky robes of grave authority
Do words put on, and in the library
The volume takes its seat among its peers,
Or quasi-peers. Nowhere such solemn shams
As pen and printer's ink can make! Man's tongue
Is flexible, but eye, face, voice, and gesture,
Body and whole demeanour help you well
To check or to corroborate his speech
(Put faith in physiognomy!); a Book
Wears deep disguise; may be a puppet-thing,
And not a man at all. The World of Books
Is full of glamour; evil, good, false, true,
Living and dead; enchanted wilderness
Where many wander, few can find a path,
Or gather what is good for them. My Boy,
I vow, shall not begin to read too soon!
Learning can nourish Wisdom, when good food
Is quietly digested; but, too oft,
Unfit, ill-cook'd, or overloaded meals
Lie crude and swell the belly with wind, or breed
Dull fat, mistook for portliness and strength.
And surely never since the world began
So many Learned Fools as now-a-days,

Or Learned Folly with so loud a voice.
Even the Wiser slip from sanity
At times, and swell the roaring storm of words.

I am your Oracle and Prophet now,
Young Mortal, weak and ignorant as I am
And fain to question rather than reply.
Yet have I journey'd on the road of life
Full many a mile, and bought experiences,
Have seen, done, joy'd and suffer'd, with a soul
Not timid, neither hard, sincere in grain,
Open to every influence, not engross'd
Of any, wishing well to all I met.
On foot, but not a beggar, have I fared,
Rested in huts and inns and palace halls,
Conversed on equal terms with many men,
Crept through dark valleys, climbed the mountain-
   tops,
And known all kinds of weather. Here I sit
By fireside, with a baby on my knee.
A Boy with golden curls and grave blue eyes,
Asking me questions. Shall I tell him truth?
Yes, Dearest, now and ever! But to know
The needful questions is to be mature.
A child but asks as prompted—and alas
Mostly by Ignorance in Wisdom's mask;
She uses words unmeaningly, and crowds
Life's pathways with memorials of man's folly.
Prompt him I must, and honestly give answer.
"Who made the world?—(Sweep widely both your arms)

c

GREAT GOD, my son · this name we call Him by.
(Lift up your eyes and little hands to him.)
How do we know Him? In the heart and soul.
(Put this hand on your brow, that on your breast.)
What is He? (Place both hands across your eyes,
And bend your head.) No man hath power to
    know."
This is enough to tell him at the time.

Man hath no thoughts to think what GOD is like,
And much less words to say; but he can feel
At times the Presence great and wonderful
Beyond all words and thoughts and dreams, and yet
Wherein we live and move and have our being.
All great truths are incomprehensible;
Much more the Living Centre of them all.
The clearest moments of the noblest men
Give insight thitherward, and what they see
Belongs to man, though some regard it not.
Soon the clouds roll together, the ground-fogs
Grow thick, and all the vision disappears;
But what the best eyes at their best behold
Is Truth Divine; the test whereof is this—
A lofty sanity of thought and life
In whoso doth receive it, harmony
Felt in his inmost being, nor wholly hid
From other men. But O impossible
To put the vision into words, nor weave
Therewith a snare! O folly, to suppose
That speech, however wonderful it be,

Is more than makeshift ! Could I stop thine ears,
Till thou art somewhat ripened in thy mind,
My son, from all more free discourse of God,
Dogmatic, controversial, personal,
I would ; and I will do it, all I can.

   It may be thou art born to a troublous time,
Retributive on nations for their sins,
Of darkness, earthquake, storm, an evil time.
At least, thou shalt escape one evil thing—
My Evil May-day, doleful to endure,
Sad to remember. Yet it pass'd ; I live ;
And GOD lives.

EVIL MAY-DAY.

Part III.

AND God lives. Yes, begin and end with that.
   For, whichsoever way you turn your face
And journey through th' illimitable vast,
You come to Nothing or you come to God.
  "We come to Matter," you reply, "more Matter,
Matter in many forms, ourselves being of them.
Man too is made of world-stuff."
                         Which contains
No mind, affection, moral principle,
Or ruling will; yet breeds them in its dance
Of purposeless gyration, turns (O strange!)
At last to speculation on itself,
And finds at choice, dust or divinity.
—I say, we come to Nothing, or to God.
  'Confront us then with Him. Who sees his face,
Or hears his voice? They told us in our youth
He paced a garden, spoke from a certain hill,
And wore a man's true body for a time.
They painted Him, an Old Man propt on clouds,
A Young Man, flowing-hair'd, with aureole,
Walking on water, flying through the air;
Much wondrous, much familiar circumstance.
But all this fading into fairy-tales,
What have we?'

     Truth. And know this well, once more,
Every high truth is inexpressible,
And God, the highest, absolutely. Men
Strive after some conception, symbol-wise,
But make too oft the symbol into idol;
And all these idols forged by human brain,
Better or worse, and aiding more or less,
Misleading less or more, long-lived or short,
Are perishable things. The idol falls;
And then it seems the pillars of the world
That break, the roof of heav'n that crashes in.
A little cloud of dust was in our eyes;
Look up: God sits enthroned, thy lord and king;
Look round, His earth is wide and beautiful.
If once thou hast that vision, treasure it,
Speak little of it, let it nourish thy life
In fair thoughts, just deeds, and self-harmony,
While the unceasing noise of human talk
Goes by, unheeded, and the multitude
Concerns itself with whatsoe'er it will.
Jove's thunderbolt, Apollo's fiery car,
Being phrases put aside, seems solar force
Less wonderful, or th' all-pervasive thrill
Of electricity? The human mind
And moral laws, do these depend on names?
The world is wider, deeper than our thought;
We walk as if in twilight: but, at times,
How, whence, we know not, all is lighted up,
Transfigured. What is shown to us? A glimpse
Of inmost truth.

        So and not otherwise
Poetic and religious thoughts are born,
Nor else interpretable. This great Light,
More glorious than the sun's, this Divine Stream,
This emanation from the Life of Life,
Named or not named, and fitliest received
With silent joy, these cloudless blissful hours
Or moments, who shall hope to represent?
The finest mesh of words being all too coarse,
The loftiest tones of poem or of creed
But distant echoes of the vibrant Soul
Throbbing and pulsing in its bath of Light,
Fill'd with the presence of the Living God,
One Power evolving multiformity,
Pervading and transcending every form.
  Such vision you may keep, or you may lose.
And what destroys it, or prevents it? This—
The setting-up False Vision in its place,
By obsolete pretended evidence,
Untrue in fact, impossible in kind,
Still palm'd on innocent souls when full of trust
And love and wonder. Once these holy names
And emblems meant what now they cannot
    mean,
As well thou knowest; yet thou teachest them
For absolute truth to tender longing souls,
Fastening their faith, their highest faculty,
To forms decay'd, worm-eaten through and through.
Vile coward! murderer of thy children's peace,
Preparing for them sick and crooked lives,

The end perhaps despair. But God's light shines,
Though men shut out, discolour, distort the ray.
   Man, in a sense, makes God. In the same sense
Man makes the World: his world is what he makes it.
Each man his World, his God. But tell me now:
The natural, true, and most miraculous World,
Which no man ever saw, can ever see,
The Living Absolute Eternal God,
Whom no man ever saw, can ever see,—
Do these depend on how a man shall think
Or picture them, or any set of men?
The God a man hath made he may pull down;
The World a man makes alters with himself;
The true, the everlasting Life remains,
Surest of all things,—personal, universal,
Ineffable, incomprehensible,
Perceived, received, as with the flower of the soul.
God rules us whether we take heed or no.
'Tis duty less than privilege and joy
To recognise Him; nor such boon to all
In equal measure. Judge its potency
In the few most receptive, not the crowd.
   Were all born blind, then who would guess the
     light?
All deaf, then who imagine any sound?
And many see the light who nothing know
Of the Sun's greatness, only dimly see
The beauty it gives birth to; many have ears
And yet by music's magic no more touch'd
Than carven figures by the organ-storm

Shaking their substance atoms.   Must thou gain
These other men's impossible consent
Before thou tremblest to the mystic joy
That frees thy spirit with a gift of wings
In Music's atmosphere ? or give account
To them of how and why thou thus art moved
By Beauty, natural or interpreted ?
Doubt, or distrust, or disbelieve, since some
With ears that hear not, eyes that cannot see,
Bring scales to measure and weigh your conscious-
    ness ?
Nay, know'st thou Love ?—a Love sublime and pure,
The world's transfiguration, through thy soul's.
If thou hast ever been assured of this,
Shall icy hearts or sneering tongues convict
High Love, and not themselves, of foolishness ?
Consider then : if that most glorious Power
Far beyond audible and visual sense,
Felt at the inmost of thy soul of souls
In moments clear and rare, at other times
Be thickly veil'd from thee or quite obscured,
Wilt thou accept the bright hour or the dark
To teach thee truth ?   If certain other men
Deny the vision wholly, wilt thou choose
Negation for thy having ? and because
Of the great glory and wonder of the light
That shone upon thee, say it was a dream,
No truth at all ?   Forget Him if thou wilt.
Deny Him.   Thou art free.   Nor will He strike
With angry flash ; not so the world is made.

No penalties are set for unbelief,
Except the natural and inevitable
Contain'd in not believing. Count these nothing,--
Who shall refute, gainsay thee? go thy ways;
The loss is in thyself; and if unfelt,
The greater. Even as the man devoid
Of music misses nothing, loveless man
Pines not for lack of love, so he to whom
This world is empty of Divinity
From earth's dark centre to the Milky Way,
Sees his world full as other men's, and seems
To live in the same world. O marvellous!
Here walk two human creatures side by side:
But seest thou in what kind of world each moves?
Not with the bodily eye. Each makes his own,
And counts his own the only. To but few
Is given the Poet's, Prophet's ecstasy;
Yet theirs the witness we accept at last.

Many are dull and scarcely heed at all.
But some turn all to question:—'What is Life,
This marvel of all marvels? Show to us
Without delay, Whence, How, and What it is,
Or must we not affirm it meaningless?
At most, a puzzle fit to stretch our wits,
The whilst we eat, drink, fight, laugh, propagate,
And play at reason, virtue, and so forth?
Guess it a dustheap, somehow grown alive,
Or else a sort of mental phantasy?
Surely, if we can't sift things, we have right

To rate them as we choose.'   There wisdom spoke.
What peevish fools, what froward babes are we!
But this at least is true beyond a doubt,—
Man's Life *has* meaning, else the world has none,
This Universe is but a puff of smoke
Floating in whirls about the gulf of space,
We atoms in the midst, and all our thoughts
Are less than nothing.
                      What Life is, I know not,
Nor claim the right to know ; but gladly accept
The highest hints and intimations given,
As likest truth.   I know not what God is,
Nor count it reasonable to suppose
A man could know ; but that God lives and rules,
My soul in times of pure and tranquil vision
Sees without effort ; which great central truth
Sways into order all the world of thought,
That else were chaos.   And, since I am I,
To me, a person, He, a person, lives ;
A Living God, of power immeasurable,
Nature incomprehensible, and plans
Inscrutable ; of whom I know by faith ;
A reasonable and necessary faith
Correlative to ignorance, and yet
No way self-contradictory, a clue
In a prodigious labyrinth, a lamp
In a great darkness

                      Why no more is known?
Enough it is the nature of things ; and how

In sooth could I conceive it otherwise,
Create a different world ? What use this faith ?—
What use wide-sweeping universal thoughts ?
Nay what use is the universe itself ?
At least we'll take for granted it exists,
Though questions may lack answers ! 'Matter,'
    'Spirit,'
What may these be ? one thing, or separate ?—
I care not which ; for how should that concern ?
All is, of need, connected, up and down,
And grossest link'd with subtlest. We must live
In a material world, must therein work,
Thereby be wrought upon. I am conjoin'd—
This personal I, (invisible as God)—
To my own bodily organs first of all ;
Related strictly to the beast, the bird,
The blade of grass, the clod of earth, the cloud,
The faintest haze of suns within the sky.
That nearest fiery orb makes flow my blood ;
Electric ether vivifies my brain ;
And I, made up of these, who am not these,
Exist in personal being, think, enquire,
Reason, imagine, feel, and nothing know ;
But in my clearest moments I think—GOD.
Ask you, What use is Faith ? Faith is like Health ;
Which, if you have in full serene possession,
You feel it every moment of the day,
In every fibre of your frame, each mood
And movement of your mind, yet for most part
Unconsciously. Inherit health and lose it,

Then shall you know its worth. But some poor men
Have never had it, and their seeming life
Is three parts death; some fling away their share
To buy diseases, or, when sense is dull'd,
Count dulness armour, take defect for strength;
Few have full measure: O to be like them!
For health is life, tho' sickness in a sort
Lives on, and nearly all the world is sick;
And Faith is higher wider subtler health,
What ether is to air, a harmony,
A pure truth inexpressible in words,
All the great truths being measureless, and God
Greatest.

O spend not life in questions: live!
Go on thy way and find there what thou may'st.
The past is past and had its own beliefs,
To-day lies round, pours in, miraculous,
And in man's soul the springs of prophecy
Well up from their unfathomable source
Unceasingly, while he has faith in God.
Belief in God—here is the fountain-head
Of all religion, and, could that run dry
To all the human race, then human life
Were but a sandy desert full of asps.
No God—No Man. Blind matter all without;
Within, delusive shadows. Hold God fast.

May-Day was evil when I miss'd my God:
Earth, sea and sky fall'n empty of a sudden,

All the wide universe a dismal waste
Peopled with phantoms of my flitting self,
And mocking gleams chance-kindled and chance
    quench'd,
All meaning nothing.   Natural May-Day
Revived to me when I found God again;
World full of beauty and significance
Wisely and justly govern'd, and I too
Part and partaker of the wondrous whole;
Made capable to feel, enjoy, adore,
To think and reason, not to comprehend.

Manhood is Freedom,—O to use it well,
Acting upon the element where I move
According to its nature and my own,
(Obscurely folded in the germ at first,
Form'd by successive subtle acts of will)
Acting to greater purpose than appears,
Nor too much sorrowing over seeming loss
Nor anxious for security of gain,
Mild, equal-minded, fearless!   To such level
Rise I in happy hour, spring-tide of soul,
Aware, without words, and beyond all words,
That God was, is, and evermore remains;
The Living Centre of this Universe,
Itself imagined only and not seen;
Always the Centre, reach'd by various roads
From many points by many different minds.
Who move tow'rds Him, converge.   Who move from
    Him

Diverge, and wander out to lonely Space,
Where they see nothing and hear nothing, save
A hollow echo of their own voice return'd
As from the Cavern of Eternal Death.
But from the Centre, Everlasting Life
Expands and pulses in perpetual waves.

Man's property is Will; and he thereby
Can turn his face to God, change his own world;
For some things must be fix'd, and some left free.
Is there not Good and Bad? and Best and Worst?
And art thou sure there is no Heaven and Hell?
Methinks we may have foretaste of them both.

IN A COTTAGE GARDEN.

BETWIXT our apple-boughs, how clear
    The violet western hills appear,
As calmly ends another day
Of Earth's long history,—from the ray
She with slow majestic motion
Wheeling continent and ocean
Into her own dim shade, wherethrough
The Outer Heavens come into view,
Deep beyond deep.
              In thought conceive
This rolling Globe whereon we live,
(For in the mind, and there alone,
A picture of the world is shown)
How huge it is, how full of things,
As round the royal SUN it swings,
In one of many subject rings,—
Carrying our Cottage with the rest,
Its rose-lawn and its martin's nest.
  But, number every grain of sand,
Wherever salt wave touches land;
Number in single drops the sea;
Number the leaves on every tree;
Number Earth's living creatures, all
That run, that fly, that swim, that crawl;
Of sands, drops, leaves, and lives, the count
Add up into one vast amount;

And then, for every separate one
Of all those, let a flaming SUN
Whirl in the boundless skies, with each
Its massy planets, to outreach
All sight, all thought: for all we see,
Encircled with Infinity,
Is but an island.
    Look aloft,
The stars are gathering. Cool and soft
The twilight in our garden-croft
Purples the crimson-folded rose,
(O tell me how so sweet it grows!)
Makes gleam like stars the cluster'd white;
And Beauty too is infinite.

EVERYTHING passes and vanishes;
 Everything leaves its trace;
And often you see in a footstep
 What you could not see in a face.

SONNET: DAFFODIL.

GOLD tassel upon March's bugle-horn,
   Whose blithe reveille blows from hill to hill
  And every valley rings,—O Daffodil!
What promise for the season newly born?
Shall wave on wave of flow'rs, full tide of corn,
   O'erflow the world, then fruited Autumn fill
     Hedgerow and garth? Shall tempest, blight, or chill,
Turn all felicity to scathe and scorn?
Tantarrara! the joyous Book of Spring
  Lies open, writ in blossoms; not a bird
  Of evil augury is seen or heard:
Come now, like Pan's old crew we'll dance and sing,
Or Oberon's; for hill and valley ring
  To March's bugle-horn,—Earth's blood is stirr'd.

NE QUID NIMIS.

YE that love astounding phrases,
   As the fashion of these days is,
Fiery colour, fierce contortion,
Dazzle, glare, and disproportion,
Elsewhere turn you. *Ne quid nimis:*
Such the motto of my rhyme is.

THE HONEST FARMER.

HAPPY I count the Farmer's life,
   Its various round of wholesome toil;
An honest man with loving wife,
   And offspring native to the soil.

Thrice happy, surely!—in his breast
   Plain wisdom and the trust in God;
His path more straight from east to west
   Than politician ever trod.

His gain's no loss to other men;
   His stalwart blows inflict no wound;
Not busy with his tongue or pen,
   He questions truthful sky and ground

Partner with seasons and the sun,
   Nature's co-worker; all his skill
Obedience, ev'n as waters run,
   Winds blow, beast, herb their laws fulfil.

An active youthhood, clean and bold;
   A vigorous manhood; cheerful age;
His comely children proudly hold
   Their parentage best heritage.

Unhealthy work, false mirth, chicane,
   Guilt, needless woe, and useless strife,—
O cities, vain, inane, insane!—
   How happy is the Farmer's life!

SEE what lives of mortals are
  On our foolish little star!
Toils unceasing, pleasures flying,
Aspirations fall'n to sighing,
Old deceits in garbs newfangled,
Angel-wings with cobwebs tangled,
Selfish comfort, drugg'd with sense,
Ambition's poverty immense,
Tender memory, sad in vain,
Flickering hope and haunting pain,
Cries of suffering, sweat of strife,—
But where the strong victorious life?
  Perchance its deeds make little noise;
No record of its pains and joys,
Save in mystic forms enscroll'd,
Spiritual eyes behold,
Seeing what lives of mortals are
On our foolish little star.

MAN'S found by his event Not whirlwind Chance
  Blows round the mystic multitudinous dance,
But Music, heard by ear the finest touch,
Sways all in order: Wisdom's ear is such.

SONNET.

LOVE, after long exilement from my breast,
   Came as of yore last night, and gave to view
   ('Twas only in a dream) the face I knew
And loved so well. Ah me, that time was best!
O pure and perfect joy, when I possest
   Thy soul in mine, when life was love of you,
   And all the fairness of the world most true,
Love being God's truth and chief among the rest!
   Was I through ignorance or folly glad
In those lost days, not having found as yet
   The secret of the world, which drives men mad,
   With one cold poison-drop for remedy?
   Or have the Powers of Darkness gripe on me
Because I flung away mine amulet?

"WHY, yes,—we've pass'd a pleasant day;
   While life's true joys are on their way."
—Ah me! I now look back afar,
And see that one day like a star.

A SAD SONG.

LOVE once kiss'd me,
   Unfolded his wings, and fled.
Hath friendship miss'd me?
Is faith in all friendship dead?
   If a spell could summon
These phantoms that come and go,
   Of men and women,
Their very selves to show,
   I might find (alas me!)
My seeking both night and day.
   But I pass them, they pass me,
And each on a lonely way.

   Soul, art thou friendless,
A loser, sorrowful, weak?
   Life is not endless,
Death is not far to seek.
   Thou sailest ever,
Each moment, if sad or kind,
   Down the great river;
It opens, it closes behind;
   Far back thou seest
The mountain-tops' faint azure;
   Below, as thou fleest,
The ripple, the shadow's erasure.

  Why dost thou, weeping,
Stretch forth thine arms in vain?
  It breaks thy sleeping;
O drop into trance again.
  In dream thou may'st go where
Child's Island is flowery grass'd,
  Deep-skied,—it is nowhere
Save in the Land of the Past.
  Time is dying,
The World too; forget their moan;
  The sad wind sighing
Let murmur, this alone.

SLEEPY.

O LEAVE me quiet for a thousand years!
 No duties, troubles, pleasures, hopes or fears,
No sun or moon with sad returning beam,
Only a faintly glimmering world, half dream,
To faintly touch my senses: rest I would,
Forget the tangled life, the bad and good,
And everything that has been,—drinking deep
The freshness of regenerating sleep,
Ages and æons of celestial rest;
To wake—I know not when,—sleep now were best.

ART THOU LORD OF THE WORLD?

ART thou Lord of the World? Was it all made for thee,
  Child of Time, Child of Clay?
Thinkest thou, skies will ever bend o'er thee,
  Bland and friendly as those of to-day?
      Every joy its savour keep,
      Night o'erflow with happy sleep,
      Pain and sorrow shun thy roof,
      Sad Old Age keep well aloof,
      Life go smoothly on its way,
      Brain control, and hand obey,
      To-morrow be like yesterday?
      Things only wait, they only wait,
    They lie in ambush for thy fate.
    Days go, and nights go,
    Years run away, and lo!
    Now the end is coming fast
    The proud foolish dream past;
    See the brand, so brightly kindled,
    To a fading ember dwindled;
    All thy pleasures, all thy riches,
    Vanish like a dance of witches!

Is this indeed the revolt thou wert fearing,
  Child of the Infinite, Child of Hope?
Or is it the lower world disappearing
  Whilst thou art lifted to higher scope?
      Thou art gently drawn away.
      Think,—truly,—would'st thou stay?
      Nothing has been given thee yet
      So good, but better thou may'st get.

SONNET: A FLOWER (IN TIME OF WAR).

FAIR Maid of February,—drop of snow
   Enchanted to a flow'r, and therewithin
A dream of April green,—who without sin
Conceived wast, but how no man may know;
   I would thou mightest, being of heavenly kin,
Pray for us all (thy lips are pure, altho'
   The soil be soak'd with tears and blood), to win
Some ruth for human folly, guilt, and woe.

A flitting phantasy and fond conceit!
   Yet mark this little white-green bell, three-cleft,
   And muse upon it. Earth is not bereft
Of miracles; lo, here is one complete:
   And after this the whole new spring-time left,
And all the roses that make summer sweet.

DENY not Love and Friendship, tho' long and vainly sought;
Thy sad perpetual craving with deepest proof is fraught.
Thou canst be friend and lover; else why thy longing now?
Canst *thou* be true and tender?—of mortals, only *thou*?

NEWS FROM PANNONIA.

A.D. 180.

DRUSILLUS.   PROBUS.

Dru. HAIL, Probus!
Pro. Hail, Drusillus!—thou in Rome!
Hale too, by Hercules! Art sick, or wounded?
  Dru. Neither, my Probus. From Pannonia, I;
A twelve days' journey. Now the Senate cons
My message, and I hurry to the bath.
Farewell, my friend; I'll visit you to-morrow.
  Pro. Nay, at this hour the public bath is throng'd,
And lo, my house at hand, and yours away
Beside the Vipsan Columns. Come, Drusillus,
Welcome awaits you, bath and robe and supper,
Not laid for guests, but large enough for two;
And then, for March wind scours the dusty streets.
Home in my litter. Bravely said, old friend!
I will not ask your camp news, well content
To hear with Rome: we'll talk philosophy,
As many a night before—dispute, agree,
And taste again the likeness in unlikeness
Friendship is mix'd of.
  Dru. Thou may'st ask my news.
All Rome, indeed, will shortly ring with it.
  Pro. Another victory and triumph? Nay,
Not a defeat? Why look you at me thus?

Dru. Cæsar ——
   Pro.   Is dead?
   Dru.   He is.
   Pro.   Aurelius dead!
O friend, a weighty message in two words!
So heavy hath not fall'n into mine ear
Since when, a youth, I heard men whispering
"Good Antoninus is no more!"—How long
Is that ago?—He was thy father's friend
I think, Drusillus, as Aurelius thine.
   Dru. He was.—Exactly nineteen years this
     month.
My father was that captain of the guard
Who came to Antoninus, lying sick,
For the night's watchword, and the Emperor,
Fixing his mild majestic eyes on him,
Said "*Equanimity.*" At dawn of day
My father saw th' imperial face again
Pale, silent, and with eyes for ever closed.
And now his great adopted Son hath join'd
The shadowy multitude. No Quadic spear
Dethroned him; it was fever's poison'd arrow
Flying invisible through the camp. He shared
The legionaries' food and long fatigues,
And every chance of war.
   Pro.   Thou too, Drusillus,
Or I mistake thee. Therefore do not scorn
This amber liquor from my own hill-slope;
Thou hast sat beneath the vines there. As thou
     wilt.

Himself was not more temperate. Was his age
Twelve lustra?
    Dru.   Save a year.
    Pro.   .   Too short a life!
    Dru Aurelius thought not so. He ask'd my age
One day, and when I told him, "At two-score"—
He said—"a wise man knows what life is like,
And, though he lived a thousand years, would see
Old things in new masks merely. Why not die?
I soon shall notch a third score on the stick,
Nor wish the game spun wearisomely out
The Roman death," he said, "a man's free choice,
Is rational, bold; great men have chosen it;
But I for my part rather will await
Th' appointed hour of natural release,
Patient of life, not fearing death at all;
A sentry at his post."
    Pro.   Go on, Drusillus!
    Dru. "Why," said the Emperor, "should death
      be dreadful?
Since it is nothing but a natural change,
One other needful movement in a world
Where all things always move, and nothing stays,
Yet nothing is destroy'd. Why shrink from change?
That Power which governs all things, changes all,
And makes from out their substance, other things,
From these things others yet, continually;
And by the flow of this perpetual change
Keeps universal nature always young."
    Pro. Thy memory's good.

Dru.   I noted down his words.
"The world, could'st thou but see it, would be seen
Shifting incessantly, but nothing lost,
And the great Whole continuing: the Gods
Also continuing, as I well believe."
   Pro. Would that we might have clearer news of
      them!
In Rome, as well thou knowest, many men
Scoff at the Gods and count them fables merely.
What would they say to this? 'Assuredly
Cæsar must keep the temples up!'—or else,
'Old-fashioned! Out of date!'
   Dru.   But here indeed
No Pontiff spoke: for one thing stay'd with him
Since Verus was his name, and Hadrian
Who loved the boy call'd him *Verissimus*;
From youth to age, truth was his very nature.
Nor custom nor tradition master'd him,
All was digested in his mind, which took
Its proper nutriment; nor he the fool
To think, like many, truths wear out with time—
Being more substantial than the sea and land.
   Pro. I trust his moderate and measured phrase
Beyond all flourishes.
   Dru.   He hated those.
"The Gods," he said, "we name them as we will:
They stand above my knowledge: but I feel
A Power Divine within me and without
Whereby all things are govern'd, changed, preserved."
And on another day these words were his:

'All from the Gods is full of Providence,
Nor Fortune separate from Nature; all
Being interwoven in one mighty web.
Why therefore should I fear to quit the earth,
If this be so? And if it be not so,
Why should I care to live in such a world,
Empty of Gods and void of Providence?"

Pro. Wise words!—and here no trivial theorist,
But Roman Cæsar, mightiest of men.
What will his son be like?

Dru. As the Gods please.
High man or low man, wise man is the man.
Marcus himself would many a time declare,
"Great Alexander, Julius, and Pompeius,
Count I but small, if match'd with Socrates,
Or Heraclitus, or Diogenes,
Or that Greek Slave."

Pro. Ay, noble Epictetus.
Aurelius would have made that slave his friend.
But let us talk of Commodus awhile.
Where is he?

Dru. In the camp. Aurelius turn'd
By nature to philosophy. He said
"The Senate gave me empire, not desired,
Much better loving shady silent paths
Of peaceful meditation, than to roll
On dusty highway in triumphal car.
But all things moved together to that end,
Adoption, training, much experience gain'd
In public functions, most of all the wish

Of him my more than father; and with these—
The driving-wheel of all—sense of man's place
And work, as social and for general use."
 Pro. A noble nature!
 Dru.   Well brought-up withal.
He loved to praise his tutors—"Thanks to them
For what I am." But he was ever humble.
"I know," he said, "being prince, and train'd thereto,
I've miss'd much man-lore simple men have gain'd
Simply, as husbandmen grow weatherwise
And fishers wary."
 Pro.   There is truth in that.
Alp sees not close but wide. Nor can the great
Well know the teasing troubles of poor men.
Was he a bookish man?
 Dru.   His books were few
I've heard him say, "Much reading is but vain.
In contemplation and experience
The wise man will discover what he needs,
Unmesh'd in subtleties and speculations
Thin-spun by curious busy-idle wits.
The sense of things is plain to healthy minds.
The nature of them deep beyond all ken;
Of qualities we learn; of essence nothing;
Nor do I deem, in myriad years to come,
Though many little truths they pick or delve
And put in storehouse, men are like to know
One atom more of Life, Death, or the Gods
Than we do now; nor shall they profit much
In happiness, perchance, by all they learn.

To view the daily earth and nightly heavens,
Feeling their beauty and magnificence;
To know there's good and evil, choose the good;
Let reason govern thee, not appetite;
Learn to be true, just, diligent, and brave;
Count all men brothers, work for general use.
Obey God, help men, and be not perturb'd,
Taking thy lot with equanimity;
These are the main things, and must always be;
What more we add, not much, though we should set
The sun and moon in scales, see the grass grow,
And fly with better than Icarian wings
From Rome to Thule."

Pro.   Had he any guess
Of how the world was made?

Dru.   "Too deep for thought,"
He said, "much more for language." Yet he mused
And question'd thus, "The nature of the Whole
Moved, and began the order'd Universe;
And everything must be continuous
From that prime impulse. Shall we deem this force,
Ev'n in the highest things whereto it tendeth,
Void of a rational principle?—or all
From one divine inscrutable First Cause,
Whence too our rational being must derive
Its powers? The order that subsists in thee
Is under rule of reason. Can this rule
Be absent in the Universe? Not so.
One Living Mind rules all."

Pro.   Remember'd well!

I see this as I never saw before
His words are precious gems.   Doth Commodus
Set forth at once to Rome?   What think'st thou of
    him?
The slaves are out of hearing.
   Dru.   Grant me this,
Dear friend, no word of politics to-night!
   Pro. So be it.   Tell me more then of our Prince
Who now is with the Gods.
   Dru.   Oft in his tent
Or by a watchfire on the battle-field,
I saw him take a little parchment-scroll
Out of his bosom; and on a certain night
He let me look therein, close-writ in Greek;
Saying, "I put these thoughts upon my tablets
As they came to me, wrote them fairly out,
And turn to them again from time to time;
Since what is written, even by oneself,
Becomes a force, takes place in the world of things,
And may be found again and scann'd again;
Thus wise mood and clear insight come in aid
Of weak dark moments, and hold judgment firm.
The most," he said, "were written long ago;
I read in them my brighter healthier self;
Now, things grow wearisome, and seldom seem
Worth the style's labour—yet are they no worse,
No better than of old."   With leave, I conn'd
The sentences, and copied many down
In our own tongue, from memory.   Words are
    seeds.

Here is my scroll, if thou art not yet tired.
But much he spoke was to the same effect.
   Pro. Nay, read, Drusillus.
   Dru.   Thus Aurelius:
"Whate'er it be, this Universe,—myself
Am part thereof, related intimately
To other parts like me, my fellow-men.
Let me be thankful and content, and seek
The common good; for happy he alone
Who, wise in contemplation, just in action,
Resigns himself to universal nature,
Expecting, fearing, and disliking nothing,
And puts his ruling faculty to use.
Ask this—how doth the ruling faculty
Employ itself? All else is but as smoke."—
"What is this hubbub that goes on around?
Vain pomp and stage-play, weapon-brandishings:
Sheep following sheep (poor men!), herds driv'n
    along,
Dogs rushing to a bone, fish to a crumb,
Labours of ants, hurry of frighten'd mice,
The posturing of puppets pull'd by strings!
View it all quietly, good-naturedly,
And not with scorn; but clearly understand
A man is worth so much as that is worth
He busies himself in. Yet, all are brethren:
Turn not away from any man or thing."—
"Wrong-doers must be, therefore marvel not
To meet one; he's in error; on thy part
Seek to amend him kindly: if thou'rt anger'd

Give thyself blame, not him. Be not perturb'd.
If a man hate thee, that is his affair,
Thine, that he have no cause. Upon thyself
Depends thy happiness; thy will is free;
Obey the voice of God."—Mark this, my friend:
" If God hath planned it all—enough. art thou
Wiser than God? But certain men surmise
Chance ruleth all, or Fate · be thou at least
Not rulèd so, and having cared for this,
Be tranquil." Note that, Probus—" Thou at least
Be not so ruled." Often would he say,
" What is the dearest, most essential thing
Whereof no man rob us? Our Free-Will!"

 Pro. A grand word! But, how choose therewith?
 Dru.   He held,
That, as our lungs inhale the atmosphere,
A subtler spiritual force pervades the world,
Which he who wills may draw into his mind.

 Pro. Strange!—yet my soul breathes freer at his
  words.
Read on.
 Dru. In this the perfect Stoic speaks:
" Rule thy opinion, and thou rulest all
Comes from without; esteem that as it is,
Nothing—the Ruling Faculty untouch'd."

 Pro. I am too weak for that!
 Dru.   Again he writes:
" Value not life at any costly rate.
Reflect: the Past a dream, the Future nothing,
The Present is the only thing thou hast,

Therefore the only thing which thou can'st lose,
And what is that?—a point."
    Pro.   The sophist here
Methinks, Drusillus—subtlety for wisdom!
The Past is *in* the Present, and the point
Is moving, therefore measureless.
    Dru.   Well said!
No man is always right.
    Pro.   And then, "Opinion?"
Suppose at some bad inn I drink sour wine,
How shall opinion make me taste and feel
Falernian? Or should angry Neptune toss
My wretched body, hath opinion power
To comfort me?
    Dru.   Some men are tougher made
No doubt, than others; for the perfect Stoic
Too nice a palate is unapt, too weak
A stomach; yet the main point lies not here.
Make by our Ruling Faculty the least
And not the most of adverse accident,
The best and not the worst of all our gifts,
We're followers, though with feeble step it be,
Of Zeno, Epictetus, and Aurelius.
Live but to gratify our lower selves
And study these, we're on the hateful road
With Nero and his parasites.
    Pro.   A gloss
On Stoicism!—a good one I allow.
I fear I'm of the sons of Epicurus—
The later sons, degenerate from his doctrine!

Dru. Nay, thou malign'st thyself—in vain to me.
No two men are alike, nor no two Stoics.
But here are maxims fit for every man·
"Act as thy nature leads, observing justice.
Rate everything according to its value.
Bear what the common nature brings to thee."
"Study not what thy neighbour says, does, thinks.
But live thine own life rightly. Talk no more
Of how a man should live, but so live thou."—
"The Soul's a sphere, and keeps her proper shape
If not stretch'd forth to outward things too far,
Contracted inward, sunken, or disperst."—
"Seek imperturbably to live a life
Of wisdom, justice, temperance, fortitude;
Be ever friendly, mild, benevolent;
And follow thy eudæmon—God within thee"

Pro. Gold words! The sweetest of the Stoics, he.
Unless it were his Father.

Dru. Nay, for him
Good life sufficed, without philosophy.

Pro Little have I of either! But note this:
Marcus's nature, that was rational,
Mild, kind and sociable; the voice within
Counsell'd him good not evil things. We all
Are not so made. Some men are idly given,
Care but for feasts and flowers and fluteplayers;
Why should they baulk their fancies? Others thirst
For glory, praise, and power; and why not seek them,

Such being their nature? How fit every man
To Marcus?
 Dru.   Ay, or any other pattern?
I said, no two alike, each his own life;
And yet must none live solely for himself.
The idle and the grasping miss true life,
Through error; help them; for, as Plato wrote,
Willingly is no soul deprived of truth;
Count all amendable.
 Pro.   Nay, some I know
In whom a cacodæmon surely whispers!
How deal with these?
 Dru.   Shun, guard against, repress,
At utmost need, expunge them solemnly,
As curs'd by fate or their perverted wills.
Aurelius could be stern—but ever sadly.
Yet, tho' in his self-judgment strict, and all
That touch'd the State, to other men at times
(Perhaps because he did not rate them high)
And women, he was far too mild, too easy;
His only fault. Witness his former colleague.
Witness his —— But enough. His life was pure,
His death was tranquil. May our souls tread firm
To follow his!
 Pro.   Alas, I would the Gods,
My Drusus, plainlier spoke to us poor men
On life and death! How should our souls be firm
When oracles are doubtful? Will new Cæsar
Follow the fierce Bellona's flashing helm?
 Dru. Not if he hold his father's counsel dear.

"Jove grant my son," Aurelius used to say,
"Have little need and no desire of war.
War I detest. Yet I have lived in war,
To keep Augustus Cæsar's legacy,
Our empire's bounds, unbroken—on the west
The Atlantic Ocean, on the north the Rhine
And Danube, with Euphrates to the east,
Africa's burning deserts to the south;
The savage isle of Britain join'd to these
By later outpulse of imperial force,
And Hadrian's Dacia afterwards. War—war—"
Would he exclaim, "I hate war—could not shun it!
O happy Antoninus, fitly named
The Pious, three-and-twenty peaceful years
The lifting of thy sceptre sway'd the world,
No further journeying than Lanuvium!"

 Two months ago, as many times before,
He spake in this wise, and on that same evening
Came I for orders to the Emperor.
And found him pacing lonely on the bank
Of the broad Danube in a wintry dusk.
My business done, he lifted up his eyes,
And seeing great stars rising in the east,
"Think of the courses of the heavens," he said,
"The boundless gulf of past and future time,
And what our little lives are. This whole Earth,
We move upon, is but a point." He stept
Silent some way, then stopping short exclaim'd—
"Who can believe that good and noble souls,
The highest things we wot of, when they leave us

Perish and are extinguished, or that God
Will not preserve them, if the general scheme
Allow thereof? This body is not me;
'Tis but the vessel and the instrument
Of an imperishable essence; yea,
Myself and God are under one same law."
He ceased; then added in a lower voice—
"Shall man dispute with God? O reverence
    Him,
Confide in Him who governs everything!
The perfect living Being, good and just
And beautiful, who generates, who holds
Together all things, who contains them all,
Continually dissolved and reproduced,
Himself not changed; from whom the soul of
    man
Is drawn, an efflux of the Deity."
When next I saw Marcus Aurelius,
He lay in fever.
  Pro.   Did it long endure?
  Dru. I'll tell thee, Probus. On the fifteenth day
I watch'd him, kneeling by the couch. His mind
Had wander'd, but he now lay motionless,
As in a trance, from noon till the fifth hour.
All unexpectedly, he look'd upon me.
Forth came his hand. I kiss'd it. My heart leapt
With a pang of fleeting joy. He merely said—
"Farewell, Drusillus. Bear the news to Rome."
Then his eyes closed again, and no more words.
  Pro. Young Commodus, I think ——

Dru.   I think, my friend,
He had a virtuous and most noble Father.
    Pro. Truly. And I for my part recollect
Caligula's father was Germanicus,
Domitian's Titus. But—Hail, Commodus!
Cæsar and Emperor, seventeenth in count
From shrewd Augustus—some amongst them great
And many vile. Fortune hath strangely throned
Pernicious human monsters, gorging blood
Until it choked them.
    Dru.   Yea, but Rome endures,
Jove's oak, whereon some carrion vultures perch'd;
Empire that was, and is, and will be great;
Never before so powerful and so happy
As under Trajan, Hadrian, Antonine,
And our beloved Aurelius.
    Pro.   And yet,
All things, Drusillus, have their term. Jove's oak
Rock-rooted, wide-arm'd, after many years
Grows hollow, one day crumbles. Shall men see
Great Rome a ruin?
    Dru.   Choose more lucky words,
Dear Probus!—or indeed wilt thou forebode
This Christian superstition, the crush'd worm,
Lord of our seven hills, with superber shrine
Than Jove's own temple now? or dost thou fear
The Britons may outrival us in arms,
Wealth, power, and policy, and one day build
A greater city than on Tiber's banks
By some cold fenny river of the north?

Pro. Nay, I love Rome.   Live Rome!

Dru. She'll outlast *us*,
Be who will Cæsar.   May the Gods protect her!
Thanks and farewell, my friend!

Pro. The slaves await you.
Health and sound sleep, Drusillus!   Fare thee well!

SONNET. A NURSERY RHYME FOR THE ELDERS.

THE Masters of the World when we are gone
   Play round our knees, look up to us with awe,
   From our lips take their earliest deepest law:
In jest we mould the clay that turns to stone,
Give little care what sort of seed is sown,
   What weeds therewith, or venoms. If we saw
The Future, with our part distinctly shown,
   Vulture Remorse might tear us, beak and claw.

Dolt! Coward! Rogue! must Ages yet to be
   Inherit, with Life's necessary griefs,
What thou thyself perceivest base in thee?—
   Factitious crimes and duties, sham beliefs,
   Pride like a murderer's, pleasure like a thief's.
Man's very best besteep'd in falsity!

THE FUNERAL.

SAY not we "bury him;" nor talk
    Of "sleeping in the grave."
With foolish words we bind and baulk
    The soul, and make it slave.

The mystic form whereby we knew
    Our parent once, or friend,
Let this, indeed, have reverence due
    For life's sake, though at end

But this no more is man at all,
    Mere water now and clay,
Fit to be purged by fire, or fall
    Apart in slow decay.

Life—Death—are hieroglyphics, writ
    By one mysterious hand;
Their meaning passes all our wit,
    We may not understand.

Forget men's timid vain pretence,
    Forget their babbling speech;
Trust to thy Spirit's highest sense
    The truest faith to reach.

NO FUNERAL GLOOM.

NO funeral gloom, my dears, when I am gone,
    Corpse-gazings, tears, black raiment, grave-
        yard grimness;
Think of me as withdrawn into the dimness,
Yours still, you mine; remember all the best
Of our past moments, and forget the rest;
    And so, to where I wait, come gently on.

THIS patchwork world of things confus'dly named,
    What voice a frank account thereof could give
And not be almost for a devil's blamed?
    Dear trusting eager Spirits, how shall I
    To your incessant questionings reply?
Children! they make me heartily ashamed
        That we amid such rubbish-mountains live,
    And true horizons hardly can espy.

A WEEK-DAY HYMN.

ALMIGHTY Plutus! Lord of Earth,
   And Giver of all Good,
Thou who hast bless'd me, from my birth,
   With lodging, clothes, and food;

Whose glory brightens every thought,
   Inspirits every deed;
In whose great name are wonders wrought,
   Whose smile is virtue's meed;

Turn not Thy face from him who bends
   Untiring at Thy throne!
Repute and station, wife and friends,
   I owe to Thee alone.

Thou helping—man dilates in form,
   And proudly looks around;
Without Thee, he's a two-legg'd worm,
   But fit for underground.

The braggart sword, the subtle pen,
   To Thee are dedicate;
Yea, all the works and wits of men
   Upon Thy service wait.

A WEEK-DAY HYMN.

Barons and dukes are feeble things,
    At Thy goodwill they shine;
Mere vassals are the greatest Kings,
    Their fleets and armies Thine.

Before Thy footstool Beauty bows,
    And Rank is cheap as mud,
And thin as smoke the bands and vows
    Of Honour, Love, or Blood.

His body in Thy service doom'd,
    The Martyr's not afraid;
Nay, gives his soul to be consumed
    To cinders, undismay'd.

In every tongue and clime confest,
    In many shapes adored,
From North to South, from East to West,
    The nations own Thee Lord,—

Thou other and thrice-golden Sun
    That dost the world illume,
Bright'ning whate'er Thou look'st upon,
    And gilding ev'n the tomb!

O may Thy sceptre, Plutus! be
    Supreme o'er land and wave—
So bless Thou *me*, and smile on *me*,
    Thy subject, and Thy slave!

A MODERN PLEASAUNCE.

OUR Garden is full of flowers and bowers;
   But the toll of a death-bell haunts the air.
We have tried to drown it with lute and voice,
Love-songs and banquet-songs for choice,
But still it is ever tolling there;
And who can silence that dreadful bell?
   Take the grim key-note; modulate well;
Let us keep time and tune with the knell,—
Sing of mad pleasure and fierce despair,
Roses, and blood, and the fire of hell!
With pants and with sobs, with shrieks and moans,
Loud laughter mingled with dying groans;
The death-bell knolling pitilessly
Through all, our key-note,—and what care we,
In our Garden full of bowers and flowers?

AN INVITATION.

TO the Wits thus writeth Crœsus:
　Gracious Heav'n hath freely giv'n
Wealth, and now of Wit we're fain;
Clever Talker,—Thinker,—Poet,—
Come and amuse us, lull us, please us;
Let's each other entertain.
Never thwart us, never tease us;
If you do, we'd have you know it,
Men of scanty dish and cup,
Not the least bit or sup
Of our feast shall fall your way.
Come, friends, come, talk and dine,
Drink our wine, and let's be gay!
　　Thought, song, and wit,
　　　Are pretty things;
　　　With nimble wings
　　Around they flit,
Tame little birds, and gently sit
With pleasant twitter—wit-wit-twit!
Our world, the solid and the true,
Likes its decorations too,
And we embellish it with you,
When we've nothing else to do.
　So honour us, dear friends, and come,
Eat, drink, make yourselves at home;
Nothing ever do or say
Which might vex us, while you stay:
Ere you bore us, go away;
And come again, another day.

THE FIRST ENGLISH POET.

DWELT a certain poor man in his day,
Near at hand to Hilda's holy house,
Learning's lighthouse, blessed beacon, built
High o'er sea and river, on the head,
Streaneshalch in Anglo-Saxon speech,
Whitby, after, by the Norsemen named.
Cædmon was he call'd; he came and went,
Doing humble duties for the monks,
Helping with the horses at behest:
Modest, meek, unmemorable man,
Moving slowly into middle age,
Toiling on,—twelve hundred years ago.

Still and silent, Cædmon sometimes sat
With the serfs at lower end of hall;
There he marvell'd much to hear the monks
Singing sweetly hymns unto their harp.
Handing it from each to each in turn,
Till his heart-strings trembled. Otherwhile,
When the serfs were merry with themselves,
Sung their folk-songs upon festal nights,
Handing round the harp to each in turn,
Cædmon, though he loved not lighter songs,
Long'd to sing,—but he could never sing.

Sad and silent would he creep away,
Wander forth alone, he wist not why,
Watch the sky and water, stars or clouds
Climbing from the sea; and in his soul
Shadows mounted up and mystic lights,
Echoes vague and vast return'd the voice
Of the rushing river, roaring waves,
Twilight's windy whisper from the fells,
Howl of brindled wolf, and cry of bird:
Every sight and sound of solitude
Ever mingling in a master thought,
Glorious, terrible, of the Mighty One
Who made all things. As the Book declared
"*In the Beginning He made Heaven and Earth.*"

Thus lived Cædmon, quiet year by year:
Listen'd, learn'd a little, as he could;
Work'd, and mused, and pray'd, and held his peace

Toward the end of harvest time, the hinds
Held a feast, and sung their festal songs,
Handing round the harp from each to each
But before it came where Cædmon sat,
Sadly, silently, he stole away,
Wander'd to the stable-yard and wept,
Weeping laid him low among the straw,
Fell asleep at last. And in his sleep
Came a Stranger, calling him by name:
"Cædmon, sing to me!" "I cannot sing.
Wherefore—wo is me!—I left the house."

"Sing, I bid thee!" "What then shall I sing?"
"Sing the Making of the World." Whereon
Cædmon sung: and when he woke from sleep
Still the verses stay'd with him, and more
Sprang like fountain-water from a rock
Fed from never-failing secret springs.

Praising Heaven most high, but nothing proud,
Cædmon sought the Steward and told his tale,
Who to holy Hilda led him in,
Pious Princess Hilda, pure of heart,
Ruling Mother, royal Edwin's niece.
Cædmon at her bidding boldly sang
Of the Making of the World, in words
Wondrous; whereupon they wotted well
'Twas an Angel taught him, and his gift
Came direct from God: and glad were they.

Thenceforth Holy Hilda greeted him
Brother of the brotherhood. He grew
Famedest monk of all the monastery;
Singing many high and holy songs
Folk were fain to hear, and loved him for:
Till his death-day came, that comes to all.

Cædmon bode that evening in his bed,
He at peace with men and men with him;
Wrapt in comfort of the Eucharist;
Weak and silent. "Soon our Brethren sing
Evensong?" he whisper'd. "Brother, yea"

"Let us wait for that," he said ; and soon
Sweetly sounded up the solemn chant.
Cædmon smiled and listen'd ; when it lull'd,
Sidelong turn'd to sleep his old white head,
Shut his eyes, and gave his soul to God,
Maker of the World.

     Twelve hundred years
Since are past and gone, nor he forgot,
Earliest Poet of the English Race.
Rude and simple were his days and thoughts.
Wisely speaketh no man, howso learn'd,
Of the making of this wondrous World,
Save a Poet, with a reverent soul.

SONNET: IN A BOOK OF MAXIMS.

"MAXIMS" of wisdom,—minims fitlier named
   If wise in any sense; the nobler part
Of human nature sneeringly disclaim'd,
   The low put forward with malicious art!
   Chicane at court and cheating in the mart
All see; but now examine unashamed
The vanities and failings of the famed,
   The selfishness of good folk: does your heart
Not feel its cockles tickled? 'We pretend
   To nothing, you and I, we know too well
How mean we are; but just observe, my friend,
   More closely these pretentions to excel,
   And with a smile admit that, truth to tell,
You find us all poor creatures in the end!'

THE STOLEN PATH.

HIGHWAYS, byways, such are my ways,
   Parks like this I detest,
Grumble to travel on miles of gravel
   Through landscapes robb'd of their zest;
Even through the gatelodge sentry
Yields us privilege of entry,
Lets us view, in passing through,
Lawns and groves whose loneliness
Doth imprisonment express
Not freedom, rhododendron flowers
Lording it over woodland bowers,
Wandering rill damm'd up to make
A lazy languid pleasure-lake,
(Who therein doth pleasure take?)
Clipt yews; geometric beds;
All 'twixt gate and gate that spreads.

  But where is that old Pathway's line,
Which, could we find it, is yours and mine,
Free from before King Alfred's day;
A winding walk, a pleasant way,
By mead and heath, by grove and glen,
Belonging to the feet of men
Past, present, and to come; that show'd
The prospect, saved the dusty road?

  Those who already have too much
Would fain get all into their clutch;

THE STOLEN PATH.

The demon greed of robber kings
Is busy here in lesser things ;
The Path is gone ; not shut by law,
But filch'd with shameless cunning paw
And swallow'd : none at hand to dare
Beard the culprit in his lair,
The Great Man, to whose mind are known
No rights at all except his own,
Who fain would shut from every eye
Th' old landscape and more ancient sky,
Save upon sufferance. Honoured Sir,
Reflect ! Art thou indeed a cur,
A caitiff ? What, beneath the sun,
Hast thou, have those before thee, done,
To earn so huge an overshare
Of the world's good things ? Have a care,
Lest, when your Worship sits on high,
A pilferer of twigs to try,
Or casual poacher, some one cry
In accents of contempt and wrath,
" Who stole our ancient Public Path ? "
—A crime incomparably worse
Than his who merely takes a purse,
Poor devil ! with the treadmill near ;
No Magistrate, M.P., or Peer.

PER CONTRA.

THIS old hereditary ground
   Welcomes within its peaceful bound
All peaceful comers. Push the gate ·
What miles of oak and fern await
Our footsteps ; unmolested space
As fair and free for you and me
As for His Grace who owns the place,
Whose ownership is not the same
As selfishness, with finer name,—
Long live such noble dukes as he !
In lieu of herald's meagre leaves,
The grateful Fancy richlier weaves,
And doth the whole wide woodland set
For garland round this coronet.

THREE SISTERS.

THREE sisters, Charlotte, Emily, and Anne,
  Afar in Yorkshire wolds they live together,
Names that I keep like any sacristan,
The human registry of souls as pure
As sky in hermit waters on a moor,
Those liquid islands of dark seas of heather;
Voices that reach my solitude from theirs;
Hands that I kiss a thousand miles away,
And send a thousand greetings of my own—
But these, alas! only the west wind bears.
—Nay, they are gone. The hills and vales are lone
Where Earth once knew them. What is now to say?
Three strangers dead—'tis little to endure:
A crowd of strangers vanish every day.
Yet will I see those gravestones if I can.

THE ADVENTURE OF THE LAMP.

SLOW-BURNING in the cavern's depth appears
  The Talismanic Lamp which rules the spheres
Of men and spirits. Safely he hath pass'd
Swords, flames, ghouls, dragons, demons; but at last
A Phantom, like his Mother, sadly stands
Full in the destined way, with warning hands.
He pauses, he forgets, he sinks, he sleeps,—
And in Elysium his true Mother weeps.

MINE—mine—
    O Heart, it is thine—
A look, a look of love!
O wonder! O magical charm!
Thou summer-night, silent and warm!
    How is it a glance
    Can make the heart dance
Which was weary and dull before?
Hush! whisper and question no more;
Nor to wind, nor to wave, nor to starlight above
    Tell thy joy; let it rest
    Like a bird in the nest,
Fall asleep without thinking, content to be blest,
And to know that this world is divine.
    It is mine—mine—
    O Heart, it is thine—
A glance of love—of love!

I AND my Love together,
   Deep in sunny sheen;
Raiment of white innocence
   Clothed us on the green

We reclined together,
   Musing grave and sweet;
Golden air embraced us,
   Blue waves nigh our feet.

Love be my guardian,
   Dreams my heritage!
My Love and I together
   In the golden age.

———

WHO could say that Love is blind?
   Piercing-sighted, he will find
A thousand subtle charms that lie
Hid from every common eye.

You that love not, blind are ye,
Learn to love, and learn to see.
'Tis the insight of the lover
Beauty's essence can discover.

———

POESIS HUMANA.

WHAT is the Artist's duty?
   His work, however wrought,
Shape, colour, word, or tone,
Is to make better known
(Himself divinely taught),
To praise and celebrate,
Because his love is great.
The lovely miracle
Of Universal Beauty
This message would he tell.

Amid the day's crude strife,
This message is his trust;
With all his heart and soul,
With all his skill and strength,
Seeking to add at length,
Because he may and must,
Some atom to the whole
Of man's inheritance;
Some fineness to the glance,
Some richness to the life.

And if he deal perforce
With evil and with pain,
With horror and affright,
He does it to our gain;

Makes felt the mighty course,
Our courage to sustain,
That sweepeth on amain,
Of law—whose atmosphere
Is beauty and delight;
For these are at its source.

His work, however small,
Itself hath rounded well,
Even like Earth's own ball
Wrapt in its airy shell.
His gentle magic brings
The mystery of things;
It gives dead substance wings;
It shows in little, much;
And by an artful touch
Conveys the hint of all.

GREAT ANCESTRY.

WE sat within a cottage by the waves,
  Hearkening to music, voice and instrument,
That floated to the still autumnal night
Starr'd over downs and ocean; and between
Its pulses, boom'd the cadence of the sea
Surge after surge along our island shore.
  Fair the musicians, and the listeners fair.
But I, apart, not merely saw and heard
Those living faces—songs—the sea—the stars
For two majestic Shades were in the night.
Deep-sounding echoes out of England's past
Commingled vaguely with the murmuring flood:
John Milton's daughters made us melody,
And Cromwell's daughters listen'd while they sang

[*Freshwater Bay*]

AUTUMN and sunset now have double-dyed
   The foliage and the fern of this deep wood.
The sky above it melting placidly
All crimsonings to gray. No sound is heard.
The Spirit of the Place, like mine, seems lull'd
In pensive retrospection. One more Spring,
And one more Summer past, and one more Year
   Anon the distant bell begins to chime,
And calls me homeward, calls me to a home
As lonely as the forest, peopled but
With memories, and fantasies, and shadows.
These wait for me this evening. What beyond?
The silent sunset of a lonely life?

FOUR ducks on a pond,
   A grass-bank beyond,
A blue sky of spring,
White clouds on the wing;
What a little thing
To remember for years—
To remember with tears!

'ALAS, friend, since your journey was begun,
  How many have outstript you in the race!'
I have not raced at all, nor even run,
  But gone along my track at easy pace,
Look'd at the landscapes, gather'd berries, shared
  Wayfaring talk, and barter'd song and tale;
  Loiter'd to hear the lark or nightingale;
'Twas for the journey, not the goal, I cared.

"QUE SÇAIS-JE?"

OLD Michael of the Mountain, strolling past,
  Careless and quiet, now and then would cast
To right or left a penetrating look;
And gather'd waifs and strays up with a hook
Shaped like the sign of query; scrap and rag
In easy reach he clapt into his bag,
Idly assiduous, mocking his own whim
With twinkling eye, and took all home with him,
Where lazily he sorted them at last.
What skill or magic in his fingers lay,
What subtly added he, 'twere hard to say;
But somehow, this took substance as a Book
That shines where all around hath fallen dim.

EQUALITY AT HOME.

"ANTOINE," cries Mirabeau, returning gay
From the Assembly, "on and from to-day
Nobility's abolish'd,—men are men,—
No title henceforth used but Citizen!
A new thrice-glorious era dawns for France!
And now, my bath." "Yes, Citizen." A glance
Of flame the huge man at his servant shot;
Then, wallowing sea-god-like, "Antoine! more hot,"
He growl'd. "Good, Citizen." A hand of wrath
Gript Antoine's head and soused it in the bath.
He spluttering, dripping, trembling,—"Rascal!
    know"
His master thunder'd as he let him go,
"For you I still remain Count Mirabeau!"

A REMINISCENCE OF THE ISLE OF MAN.

ONE April found me upon Mona's shore,
With daily prospect of the Cumbrian Hills,
Cloud-wreathed or sunlit, o'er the Irish Sea.
"A Man dwells there; and one day I shall walk
Through landscapes that confess him suzerain

Under the SOVEREIGN LORD of earth and men,
May see the Prince himself, may humbly meet
His venerable eye, may hear his voice."
And day by day new Spring upon the fields
And waves grew brighter.
                    One day brought this word—
'The wise old Poet of the mountain-land
Is gone away for ever. You may seek
But never shall you find him any more
Among the shadows of the folded hills,
By lonely tarn or dashing rivulet,
Down the green valley, up the windy fell,
In rock-built pass, or under whispering leaves,
Or floating on the broad translucent mere
Between two heavens. You will but find his grave.'

I paced the strand, and clearer than till now
Saw the far coast across a glittering tide;
But how forlorn those faint-blue rocky peaks!
How emptied of its joy the enchanted ground!
I paced the strand, and raised mine eyes anew,
And saw as 'twere a halo round the peaks.
Something of Him abides there, and will stay.
Those Mountains were in WORDSWORTH'S soul;
    his soul
Is on those Mountains, now, and evermore.

DREAMS.

IN morning mist and dream I lay,
   And saw, methought, two Babes at play
In a green garden, girl and boy;
With Lucy painting in her chair,
The sunshine catching golden hair
At moments when she lifts her head
To look at these.—

         A dream ?—Ah woe !
This used to be, long time ago.
The Mother and the Babes are dead,
And I am old and lonely : fled
Life's pleasure now, itself a dream.

  How long a dream lasts, who can say,
Or how it drifts, and intershifts ?
I woke, I saw the sunny beam,
I heard the shrieking of the swifts,
Then flung my curtain back. Below,
Two merry faces all a-glow
Look up, "Good morning, dear Papa !
Mama is coming home to-day."

  Grant us to taste, ye Mystic Powers,
Our happy hours,—O how they haste !

VIVANT!

NO need, I hope, to doubt my loyalty;
   From childhood I was fond of Royalty;
To Kings extravagantly dutiful,
To Queens yet more, if young and beautiful.

How rich their robes! what crowns they all had too!
And yet how friendly to a small lad too!
At glorious banquets highly gracing him,
Beside the lovely Princess placing him.

Their kingdoms' names I did not care about;
They lay in Fairyland or thereabout;
Their date, though, to forget were crime indeed,—
Exactly, "Once upon a time" indeed.

And still they reign o'er folk contented, there
I hope to have my son presented there:
At every virtuous court in Fairyland,
Its Cave-Land, Forest-Land, and Airy-Land.

So down with democratic mania!
Long live great Oberon and Titania,
Imperial Rulers of those regions!—he
Be shot who wavers in allegiancy!

And bless all Monarchs in alliance with them,
Who've no enchanters, dragons, giants with them,
To keep sweet ladies under lock and key,
And answer challenges in mocking key!

BIRDS' NAMES.

OF Creatures with Wings, come now let us see
   Which have names like you and me.
Hook-nosed Poll, that thinks herself pretty,
Everyone knows, of all birds most witty.
Daw our good friend, in grayish black,
If you ask him his name, will answer "Jack!"
Bold Philip Sparrow hopping you meet,
"Philip! Philip!"—in garden and street.
Robin Redbreast perches near,
And sweetly sings in the fall of the year.
Grave Madge Owlet hates the light
And shouts "hoo! hoo!" in the woods at night.
Sweet Nightingale, that May loves well,
Old Poets have call'd her Philomel,
But Philomelus, *he* sings best,
While *she* sits listening in her nest.
Martin! Martin!—tell me why
They call you so; I know not, I;
Martin the black, under cottage eaves,
Martin the small, in sandy caves.
Willy, Willy Wagtail, what runs he takes!
Whenever he stops, his tail he shakes.
Head and tail little Jenny Wren perks,
As in and out of the hedge she jerks.
Brisk Tom Tit, the lover of trees,
Picks-off every fly and grub he sees.
Kitty Wake on the sea-wave rides,

Her nest on the lofty cliff abides.
Mag, the cunning chattering Pie,
Builds her home in a tree-top high,—
Mag, you're a terrible thief, O fie!
   Tom and Philip and Jenny and Polly,
Madge and Martin and Robin and Willy,
Philomelus and Kitty and Jack,—
Mag the rogue, half-white, half-black,
Stole an egg from every Bird;
Such an uproar was never heard;
All of them flew upon Mag together,
And pluck'd her naked of every feather!

———

I'M but a lowly gooseberry
   Hanging on my native tree
Here i' the sunshine of the garden
(For which I humbly beg your pardon)
Just within the children's reach;
Don't be angry with me, pray,
Mister Critic,—did I say,
Ever say I was a peach?

———

AMY Margaret's five years old,
   Amy Margaret's hair is gold,
Dearer twenty-thousand-fold
   Than gold, is Amy Margaret.

"Amy" is friend, is "Margaret"
The pearl for crown or carkanet?
Or peeping daisy, summer's pet?
   Which are you, Amy Margaret?

A friend, a daisy, and a pearl,
A kindly, simple, precious girl,—
Such, howsoe'er the world may twirl,
   Be ever,—Amy Margaret!

I SAW a little Birdie fly,
   Merrily piping came he;
"Whom d'ye sing to, Bird?" said I;
   "Sing?—I sing to Amy."

"Very sweet you sing," I said;
   "Then," quoth he, "to pay me,
Give one little crumb of bread,
   A little smile from Amy."

"Just," he sings, "one little smile;
   O, a frown would slay me!
Thanks, and now I'm gone awhile,—
   Fare-you-well, dear Amy!"

A MOUNTAIN ROUND.

TAKE hands, merry neighbours, for dancing the
    round !
    Moonlight is fair, and delicious the air.
From valley to valley our music shall sound,
    And startle the wolf in his lair.
From summits of snow to the forests below,
Let vulture and crow hear the echoes—O ho !
        (O ho !)
While shadows on meadows in dancing the round
    Go whirligig, pair after pair !

A MOUNTAIN ROUND.

Allegretto.

Take hands, mer-ry neighbours, for dancing the round! Moonlight is fair and de-li-cious the air; From val-ley to val-ley our mu-sic shall sound, And star-tle the wolf in his lair. From sum-mits of snow to the for-est be-low, Let vul-ture and crow hear the ech-oes, O-ho! (O-ho!) While sha-dows on mea-dows in dancing the round Go whir-li-gig pair af-ter pair!

JOHN CLODD.

JOHN CLODD was greatly troubled in his mind,
But reason for the same could noways find.
Says he " I'll go to Mary , I've no doubt,
If any mortal can, she'll vind it out."
" Why, John, what *is* the matter ? where dost ail ?
In 'ead or stummick ? eh, thou dost look pale.
Can't ait ? can't sleep ? yet nayther sick nor sore ?
Ne'er velt the like in all thy life afore ?
Why, lad, I'll tell 'ee what,—thou beest in love."

John look'd at Mary, gave his hat a shove,
And rubb'd his chin awhile, and mutter'd " There !
Only to think o' that !"—then from a stare
Broke by degrees into a smile, half-witted,
" Dang ! Mary, I don't know but what you've hit it !
I thought on no sich thing, but now I see
'Tis plain as haystack. Yaas, in love I be !
But *who* be I in love wi, Mary ? Come !"
"Why, can't yo tell that, John ? Art blind, or dumb ?
Is't Emma White ? or Liz ? or Dora Peak ?
Or pirty little Sue ? or Widow Sleek ?
Or Tilda Ruddilip ? or Martha's Jane ?
Or Squire's new Dairymaid ? or old Miss Blaine,
Wi' lots o' money ? Don't be angry, John,
I've guess'd all round,—you hates 'em every one ?
Still, you loves zumbody . . . Mayhap 'tis *me?*"

"Why, Mary, what a clever lass you be!
I never once took thought on sich a thing;
But you it is, and no one else, by Jing!"
"Well, John, that's settled; so Goodnight at last.
"No, Mary, don'tee run away so fast!
What next are we to do?"
       "What next? O bother!
Get married, I suppose, sometime or other."
"Right, lass, again! I niver thought o' that.
How do'ee iver vind out things so pat?
But stop a minute, Mary,—tell me how
Does folk— ... She's off! I'm fairly puzzled now!"

———

FAMILIAR EPISTLE TO A LITTLE BOY,
With a Book of "Songs, &c."

I MUST own, my dear Sonny, 'tis likely but few,
   Will care for this book; but I count upon you
For one reader, and hope you'll find something to
   please
And nothing to plague you in verses like these.
You've already a much truer taste in poetics
Than many grown-up folk, and some famous critics;
An "ear," which you have, is essential; but this
The people most wanting in can't even miss.
O give me the young! And at least you'll be mine;
You'll sometimes remember a song or a line
As the years travel round, as new mornings arise,
New sunsets draw softly away from the skies,
Like the old ones I saw? When your life-wheel
   shall bring
The freshness, the flutter, the ripple of Spring,
And Summer's broad glow, and grave Autumn be-
   dight
In his tarnish'd gold russet; then bareness and white,
And the clasp of sweet home in the long Winter's
   night,
With their moods and their fancies;—"As I feel, he
   felt,"
Perhaps you will say, "and was able to melt

FAMILIAR EPISTLE TO A LITTLE BOY.

Life's crudeness and strangeness, some part, into
   song,
For his soothing and mine." Dearest Gerald, so
   long
As a ghost may keep earth round him (not meaning
   clay)
This will soothe too, to fancy 'Perhaps he will say.'
Nor will that ghost be happy unless he may know
Your footsteps have wander'd where his used to go
In the young time and song-time—among those
   green hills
And gray mossy rocks, and swift-flowing rills,
On mountain, by river and wave-trampled shore,
Where the wild region nourish'd the poet it bore,
And colour'd his mind with its shadows and gleams.
That lonely west coast was the house of his dreams
And his visions,—O Future and Past that combine
At a point ever shifting and flitting, to shine
In the spark of the Present! Old stories re-sown
Sprang to life once again, became part of my own,
Like 'mummy-wheat' sprouting in little home-
   croft;
The Ladder for Angels—it slanted aloft
From our meadow; the Star in the East hung on
   high
Where Fermanagh spreads dark to the midwinter
   sky;
And the Last Trumpet sounded o'er Mullinashee
With its graves old and new. And now tenderly,
   see,

They glide forward, and gaily, the sweet shapes of
    Greece,
All natives and neighbours, for wonders don't cease;
Shy Dryads come peeping in woody Corlay,
And surge-lifted Nereids in Donegal Bay.
Olympus lay south, where the mists meet and melt
Upon Truskar. My Helicon, drought never felt;
It was Tubbernaveka, that deep cressy well.
A goddess-nymph kiss'd my boy-lips if I fell
Into slumber at Pan's hour in fragrant June grass;
Processions of helmeted heroes would pass
In the twilight; I saw the white robes of the bard
With his lyre. But the harp whose clear music I heard
Was Irish, and Erin could also unfold
Her songs and her dreams and her stories of old.
See Ireland, dear Sonny! my nurture was there;
And my song-gift, for which you at least are to care,
Took colours and flavours unfitted for vogue,
(With a tinge of the shamrock, a touch of the brogue,
Unconsciously mingling and threading through all)
On that wild verge of Europe, in dark Donegal.
—"Dark," did I say!— Is there sunshine elsewhere?
Such brightness of grass, such glory of air,
Such a sea rolling in on such sands, a blue joy
Of more mystical mountains?
                              O eyes of the Boy!
O heart of the Boy! newly waken'd from sleep.
Might I sleep again, MASTER, long slumber and deep,
To wake rested!
               But go there, my Gerald, this book

In your pocket, with fresh heart and eyes take a look,
At the poor lonely region,—ah, where will you see
The heavenly enchantment that wrapt it for me?

  In any case, Laddie, I trust you will be as
Good son as was formerly pious Æneas,
Will carry your Daddie the poet right through
This house-afire Present and hullabaloo,
And, going on calmly when forward you've bent your eye,
Set him down safe in the Twentieth Century.
Strange feels that no-when! I shiver at sight
Of a realm like the North Pole, of icefields and night!
Can the world and old England be yet living on?
Our Critics and Big-Wigs, O where are they gone?
Nay, courage! methinks one may feel more at home
By degrees there: a sweet chilly breath seems to come,
Like new Spring's, from the Future. It won't be so bad;
In fact I believe it will suit me, my lad!
We travel to new things in time as in space,
And escape out of habitude's bonds that embrace
And enjail us; we win change of air for our thought,
And that same with restorative virtue is fraught.
Though knaves, fools, and humbugs no doubt there will be,
They won't be the same we're accustom'd to see
And be plagued with. 'Tis thinking about them offends,

But the new can't take hold. Nay, respectable friends
Often bore us—the crowd of relations, connections,
Conditions, traditions, and foolish subjections;
(Small wonder if people run sometimes away,
"Without any reason," as dull neighbours say,
Who themselves are the reason, with all the routine
One got sick of)—Hurrah! change of air! change of scene!
"Number Twenty will have its own Poets, be sure,
Its own Judges"—I hope so: do fashions endure?
They flow, eddy, try back, as one often has found;
And a thing out of favour—its turn may come round;
Dear Public may long for the simple and plain
For a change, too,—sound appetite come, or again
Perhaps from a hot queasy stomach's sensations
Demanding cool drink after fiery potations.
Why care? Just because there are people, a few,
Scatter'd up and down space (perhaps more, if we knew)
Whom a flying word reaches, a force yet more subtle
And swift than the ether's electrical shuttle,
All-weaving; a shaft thrilling muscle and marrow,
Or lighting as softly as thistle-seed arrow,
To comfort, to kindle, to help, to delight;
And our brave English speech has a far-reaching flight,
(Though what may become of it soon there's no telling

With novel and newspaper, slang and misspel-
    ling),—
A mere little Song—Yes, one's hardly content
To think one's fine impulses, efforts, misspent,
All the hopes and sweet fancies but blossom and
    cloud
Of an old merry Maytime, long stretch'd in its shroud.
But enough to this tune. So *cushla-ma-chree*,
(As my nurse used to say) and dear Reader to be,
Garait ōg, may God bless thee, my own little Son !
—Look me up in the year Nineteen-hundred-and-one.

THE WINTER PEAR.

IS always Age severe?
   Is never Youth austere?
Spring-fruits are sour to eat;
Autumn's the mellow time.
Nay, very late i'th' year,
Short day and frosty rime,
Thought, like a winter pear,
Stone-cold in summer's prime,
May turn from harsh to sweet.

'NEW Heavens and New Earth,'—and must all
   be new-created?
No. One touch to *your microcosm* may do whatsoever is fated.

WHEN I was young and fresh and gay,
    Full moody oft I went;
The troubles of the passing day
    So wrought me discontent;

Those flaws and fallings-short in life
    Which every one must bear,
Oppressions, hints to rebel strife,
    Enormous wrongs they were.

Whatever man could have or be,
    Nay, every fancied boon,
Belong'd, I thought, as much to me
    As share of sun and moon!

Whom Eden could not satisfy
    Is thankful for a flow'r;
Who craved for earth and sea and sky
    Loves most a quiet hour.

To run safe through this earthly lease,
    Be kindly with one's kind,
Enjoy a little, part in peace,
    Were rare good luck, I find.